HOW TO KEEP THINGS ALIVE

HOW TO KEEP THINGS ALIVE

poems

Beth Gordon

Split Rock Press
2023

ISBN 978-1-7354839-5-5

Cover art and book design by Crystal S. Gibbins.

Split Rock Press is dedicated to publishing eco-friendly books that explore place, environment, and the relationship between humans and the natural world.

Environmental consciousness is important to us. This book is printed with chlorine-free ink and acid-free paper stock supplied by a Forest Stewardship Council certified provider. The paper stock is made from 30% post-consumer waste recycled material.

Split Rock Press Chapbook Series readers: Amy Clark, Crystal S. Gibbins, Whitney (Walters) Jacobson, Serenity Schoonover, and Natasha Pepperl.

www.splitrockreview.org/press

For C.T.

— my sibling to the wolf mother poetry

TABLE OF CONTENTS

Full of Grace   *9*

Something Is Waiting to Hatch   *10*

To the Young Poets   *11*

Full of Woe   *12*

Aubade: Between Now and Never (i)   *13*

Mutually Assured Destruction   *14*

/ Snakeroot/ Oleander / Belladonna /   *15*

The Spider in the Shower   *16*

sonnets of apology   *17*

Aubade: Between Now and Never (ii)   *18*

Incubation   *19*

I'm Inventing a New Language Redux   *20*

Something Is Waiting to Howl   *21*

Flying Doesn't Look Like Flying   *22*

Aubade: Between Now and Never (iii)   *23*

Requiem   *24*

In Which I am Dreaming About My Ghosts Again   *26*

after Uvalde   *27*

All the Things You Tried to Tell Me / All the Things I Already Know   *28*

How to Keep Things Alive   *29*

Notes   *31*

Acknowledgments   *32*

About the Author   *33*

FULL OF GRACE

You are the only other person who knows where we buried the moonshine.
You know the names we gave to dogwood trees by the creek: *lost cause,*
    foolish heart.
Which roots hold Uncle Jim's secret cornbread recipe.
Who else was there when the chickadee pair argued over twigs and dry
    moss?
When we drank coffee that smelled like strawberries in a firepit.
When the geese across the valley traded hidden codes in their rhymes.
A crate of martini glasses in the cob-webbed square beneath the stairs.
Dig deep enough and you'll find the guard dog's skeleton and deeper
    still, an unnamed cousin who carried the bullet with him: his rib cage
    like a china cabinet.
Another crate for champagne flutes and the deviled egg tray: painted
    with a bouquet of lilacs or hydrangea: we never could agree.

We murdered the line of azaleas that failed to bloom for three cold Springs.
You know their final resting place and final song.

I know where your mother's white dishes are hidden: the box labeled
    mousetraps and jelly jars.
The key to your storage unit where her green-stamp bureau resides.
I know that your thyroid function is fine this week but your hemoglobin
    levels are low.
When the doctor calls I won't ask which sin lit up your chart like a vine.
When the doctor calls I'll know: black ice or arsenic: slick pine needles:
    the layer of pollen that turned your white car as golden as a calf.
The log truck in your rearview mirror: smoking furnace: tangled electric
    lines.
Lead in the water: water in the basement.
The last drop of whiskey: flat tire on a murky mountain road.

I'm already ready for it. I'm wearing my funeral shoes.
I'm already ready for it. Your heart in a puddle by the bed.

SOMETHING IS WAITING TO HATCH

I don't know how my father's last breath sang,
whether that song like a caterpillar
spinning or a stadium imploding
in a thunder-ed release of spores & worms,
can be found in the dreams of the black cat.
The black cat dreams, I'm sure of it. I don't
know what he dreams. I can Google cat dreams.
I can Google the number of muscles
in the human body but I prefer
to believe it is endless as a bowl.
The black cat doesn't count muscles or bones.

I don't know the name of the bird who lives
in the rhododendron bush, so fractured
by purple blooms I forget to Google
his markings and the way he carries worms
to a hidden nest. Something is waiting
to hatch. The black cat doesn't know the name
of the bird but he dreams of brown wings: bones
in his claws. I don't know how many moles
are on my back. My ex-lovers may know
but I don't know where they are, not the names
of cities or avenues: phone numbers.

I know my father's muscles swam away
like fish. He had twenty moles. The black cat
is always sleeping when I walk into
a room. I don't know if he is breathing
until he opens his fiery green eyes
and speaks. I don't know what he is saying.

TO THE YOUNG POETS

Golden Shovel with Two Ad Campaigns and List of Lipstick Hues

It's impossible to explain how much everyone smoked: cigarettes between the fingers of surgeons & priests & waitresses: our mothers smoked in the middle of the day while on TV a 4-star general stood on a hill of bodies & John Dean charmed suburban bridge players. There was no warning: no one ever asked: forget the movies: the sexy/sticky cocktail lounges & Don Draper smoking while panties dropped. Our grandmothers smoked while frying chicken or on the 1st of May watering daffodils. Our teachers smoked: the school counselor: the spinster librarian. I want to be clear about this: the principal & janitor shared Lucky Strikes in the parking lot while hazardous fumes drifted into the cafeteria window where we drank milk from waxed cartons and into our stale peanut butter sandwiches. Our fathers walked down main street: through your back yard: flicked Marlboro ashes & Marlboro butts into azalea bushes: our long-term health

on nobody's mind. Best friends: arms linked around each other's waists: beautifully unaware of our bodies. Cancer everywhere: we never flinched: packed in the backseat with cousins: we didn't inhale. Camel unfiltered: sweet with my grandfather's breath: his jars of old coins: the way he walked five final steps & the moisture in his lungs pulled him under: we believed he was the last smoker to survive the 70's: the slick & cynical 80s unimpressed by his nicotine ways. One day the world was as creamy as a mushroom cloud: the next day non-smoking sections appeared like weeds: protective & unnecessary. Lab-created fruit flavors: lab created poppies: petroleum-based emollients on the road ahead: Aunt Janice left behind. Holding her lukewarm can of PBR & for good measure: ragged bathrobe: Virginia Slim menthol dangling from her painted lips:

Strawberry Brook / Red Waterlily / Coral Raincloud / Plum Storm / Rainy Rose / Sip of Pink.

FULL OF WOE

And it should not smell of honeysuckle:
wet honeysuckle bathed in black widow
webs: honeysuckle as new as cotton
candy: as white as the belly of a goose. No:
it should never sound like cardinal song:
not young cardinals or old lawnmowers
competing for the day: one to nest / one
to bury the dog's bone beneath the blade.
Turn off the rusty sprinklers: no children's
slippery soles gliding across muddy
lawns like clean swans just before flight. Bacon
should not be grilled on middle afternoons.
No fresh-picked tomatoes split open with
a rush of ripe mint and succulent seeds.
Do not spread hollandaise across your tongue
That day should not taste of lemon or fresh
eggs. And it should look as ordinary
as sidewalks, as tired as a rattle
snake at noon. Leave your sunglasses on top
of the refrigerator with the loaf
of moldy bread. All light will dissipate:
the abundant flower moon will also hide
her pink face. Swarms of grasshoppers will wait
until dawn to deny that day of green.

AUBADE: BETWEEN NOW AND NEVER (i)

Then one morning the morning grass was wet with frogs. Each small
blade a glistening. Each small root a river flush with minnows. The
morning sparrow grew un-young & silent. My love, the silence of a
sparrow is the silence of the dead. Violin strings vanished in a cloud of
seed. Each seed a feast. A million impossible wombs. A million times
my name in your mouth. A million mornings the grass was slick with
snails. Sticky with webs. The eight-legged wolves burrowing at the first
pluck of morning light. Four-legged wolves cross a bridge of forsythia
as tangled as your veins. Each vein a heart string rippling like wheat.
Each string a chorus of petals on a hummingbird's tongue. A million
tongues as brutal as stone. A million stones clamber to rise, my love.

MUTUALLY ASSURED DESTRUCTION

for Andre

Our adults were weary prophets with mouths
made of Bibles & gin. Mothers in green
kitchens learning to bake casseroles. Fathers
in the driveway: coming or going: Johnny
Cash or Johnny Rotten on the radio.
Saturday morning shoeshine. Saturday night
horror. My brother the saddest person
in the room when Godzilla burned Tokyo
down. Easter Sunday resurrection: our
familiar giant rising from a pile of lesser men.
His good hands as gentle as a reed: his good
hands like a basket cradling eggs: pastel
green: dewdrop yellow. Monday morning bus
stop with packs of belt-whipped boys. Sandwich
on the sidewalk. Winter coat beneath their feet:
milk in the gutter. There's a runaway
truck in this story. Gravel-spit. Wild-toothed.
Building snow men with butterscotch eyes.
My knees bloody from yesterday's brawl.

/ SNAKEROOT / OLEANDER / BELLADONNA

I fell out of the belly of a dandelion: I fell out of the bottom of a well:
I fell out of the clock and swallowed a nest of empty nests: a sticky
oil-slick hornet wrapped with twine inside my walls.

A bundle of love letters from the nightshade-flavored men: a long-
desired miscarriage and every floor / every ceiling / all the open
doors/disappeared like hands. I climbed into my good stomach.

I climbed into the mole beneath my pubic hair. Honeysuckle / mud
wasp / blackberry bramble / blackberry bramble. The goddess of
thistles branded me. Seed-wish. Jimsonweed. Hemlock witch.

No: in a world where men own the blackberry vines / the highway
off-ramps / fire extinguishers / ATM machines / conveyor belt
cameras / my skin is an amplifier of memory: the shrieking demon

trapped in wood grain: flower moon / ocean moon / tornado moon
/ moon: blindness disguised as salt. Temporary nausea: the
necessary purging of all that came before. Loss of feeling in face and

fingers and toes: a trio of major arcana. High Priestess. Starsong.
Death. Three days later I rose from my tiny room. What happened
on the stairs beneath the God-faced door? Crow witch. Spine

burned raw by shag carpet in 3 shades of wolf: Chrysanthemum
Orange. Bikini Yellow. Dirty Gold.

THE SPIDER IN THE SHOWER

Someone said my name today. I was standing
in the afternoon shower. While I stared at the top
of my feet, someone said my name. With a soft b
like belief or benign. No husband. No lover.
No man standing in the shower. Saying my name.
The b would have been harder in a man's mouth:
breakfast or bargain. A translucent gray spider
rappelled from the ceiling. She rewound when
the first dot of water blew by her like a fly.
Fruit flies rise from the drain. Not the drain in this
shower full of b's. They rise from my kitchen
drain. They ballerina on lemon skin.

Every morning I want to remember something
yellow. Today that yellow thing is the lemon
in the drain. The fruit flies make a sound like belly-
ache. If he were not in Vermont he would say:
believe I will never leave. Standing in the shower.
Blinded by soap. The lemongrass soap he bought
at the airport duty-free. He drained the kitchen
sink. He said see what I bring. The thing I wanted
was as yellow as God's heart. The spider clung
to a ceiling crack. I lifted a bright cloth to my skin.
Someone said my name, like a daffodil beginning.

SONNETS OF APOLOGY

i'm sorry for comparing you to new
rabbits for eight years   winter rabbit snow-
prints your undertow   face flickering like
a fluorescent ceiling light   i'm sorry
for metamorphosis metaphors   worms
swimming in the afterbirth   for tadpoles
for drownings   for losing you in my dream
i'm sorry for the colors   dolphin blue
voices far beyond the binoculars
where lightning is never seen without death
your eyes   a memory of memory
i'm sorry i've forgotten your human
fingers   the grey of empty hurricanes
for the DNA I gave you   forgive me

for losing you in my dream   for airport
voices runway lights   guiding you beyond
the weather lightning   fog that grounds all flight
i'm sorry i was wine drunk when you closed
your eyes when you hushed   your cricket chatter
to the ears of the grounded   forgive me
the listings of superstitions   simple
plagues hurricane gods heart attacks foreign
objects caught   in the swallow of sorrow
where stars disappear where   stars disappear
your bloom   a memory of memory
i'm sorry I've forgotten your tadpole
fingers   the blue of sudden dragonflies
forgive me   for the DNA I gave you

AUBADE: BETWEEN NOW AND NEVER (ii)

Then one morning the morning sky was green with wings. The morning sky an ocean of seven gods. Drowned god, rot god. Hornet god, wasp-nest god. Bleed-out god, whiskey god. The god inside my ribs. Each rib a green feather. Each feather a highway. Each highway a noose. The dead stay dead, my love. The morning requires this journey. The morning hummingbird is new-born. The evening hummingbird a furious ghost. A million ghosts beneath our bed. The bed lazy-ed with smoke. The smoke lazy-ed with lies. Each lie the heart of the hornet god. A million gods at the fiery tip of your cigarette. The flame of petal-ed highways waits beyond the door.

INCUBATION

A car drove by & you named it gray cat.
A car drove by & I named it blue heart.
I tried to see gray ash in your eyes. Fire-
pit ashes the morning after. My family
was not a camping family. My brother
& I as content as stone pigeons.
Playing pirate ship on the four-post bed.
Playing lava river while my mother
scrambled eggs. The morning after I could
not see. The birch. The shagbark. The mourning
doves. I named the car blue like a funeral
suit. You did not see the funeral. Not
the casket covered with Van Gogh's starry
night. His ashes floating like cherry
blossoms. The hearse arrived. Glimmering black
like young soldiers' shoes. As hungry as light.
You cried with me & led me over the
brewing river. You folded the tent.
The campfire a heart full of cold
embers. The sky as blue as a pigeon.

I'M INVENTING A NEW LANGUAGE REDUX

I've been counting sparrow feathers for 1800 days and I've unearthed
the love songs in the scar between my toes. Splicing consonants from
nest-twig, nouns from *proliferation*. Learning to navigate butter-thick
pronunciations of hurricane cocktails, jellyfish sonnets, jalapeno hush
puppies that dance between my teeth. I'm telling you I have oxygen
inside these aging lungs, I salivate when I smell a man with cigarette
skin. I have no need for precognition, the decibels of floods. I rise to
the present harmonies of fingernails upon my back, champagne
bubbles, something glistening in the dark. I'm finding abandoned wine
corks, the remnants of celebration, tulip bulbs exploding like rug
burns in the cool Nebraska sky, the talking rag doll my father gave me
on my third birthday, the string I pulled over and over to memorize
her rhymes. The lilac dust in the back corner of my grandmother's
lingerie drawer, a bumblebee mating dance in the lingering sunshine
of Emily Dickinson's window. I've reimagined castles of clover, of
bloom, of 3D printers, reading the instructions to redesign my DNA,
the source of my vibration in mitochondrial pairs, like the astronaut
who returned to Earth only to discover that he is now mankind's
perfect celestial double.

SOMETHING IS WAITING TO HOWL

What they will tell you of love is that
they have been hungry and wandering
their entire lives. A patch

of wild strawberries did not ease this
ache: a frozen lake, summer tornado.
They left the prayer

group/the youth fellowship retreat to
climb the mountain and hitchhike
back in time for social hour.

Some of them did not survive this: the
man in the red pickup truck with a red
bandana and a bottle

of copper-stilled gin turned down
another road. They are always walking
into the highway following

the lights of the plane. They never saw
what hit them. In this timeline they
buy you whatever you

want and let you sip whiskey from
their glass. They lived in an
abandoned bomb shelter one spring

and knit the blanket on your bed.
They didn't stay in the laundry
room/the kitchen/not in the den.

They will sleep through the coyote's
nightly howl while the men in the
house are awake. Shivering.

FLYING DOESN'T LOOK LIKE FLYING

They listen for the ladder's metallic scream,
dragging of grandmother's sheets onto roof, but instead the two-year-old simpl
thumbs down a hawk's wing while her parents
are mixing the perfect margarita on an ordinary afternoon in May.
You remind that this is the way of things,
that heartbeats are beautiful, a tailspin kind of organ that can
absorb the moon & sparrows, that the brick
house filled with antique spoon collections & porcelain dolls will
be an airport in 24 hours with the addition
of hibiscus elixir, the ritual of feather and dirt, the spell that will lift all things.
I try to remember what my teacher said about
the difference between arteries and veins, the way blood carries peppermint oil
or blackberry-infused whiskey without discrimination.
That children born on the magical edges of this planet will find within
their necessary lives the whispered footsteps
of dragonflies in half-morning rooms, the tails of cloud-bound kites, an unearth
message of witness and light, the chime
of lightbulbs, of gardens that carry them into the future of weightlessness:
uprooted, web-spun, newly divine and cacophonic.

AUBADE: BETWEEN NOW AND NEVER (iii)

Then one morning the morning door was barricaded with sand. Each grain a history of morning. Each history a song of violets & violence & currents & the moon. The morning moon as pale as a lizard belly. The lizard's tail an afterthought. The door waited for our hands. Our hands entwined like wool to needle. My love, I am the needle at your throat. My love, I am the unblinking eye of the moon. My love, this room is closing in. A million rooms that smell like your hair. A million rooms that hide the reptile secrets of our path. Each grain of sand a warning.

REQUIEM

i.

Spiders revise their death masks / their chemical
compositions when scorched with ice: cold-
hardening: this is also true of mud
frogs. Mud wasps. Mud sparrows. Running down this
mountain with Tom Petty on our tongues. Wind
chimes on a still day as lush as winter
melting. All bursting with foxglove whispers.
A travel hymn shifting to its final
chorus: unable to keep him alive:
he is the cabinet of spidery ghosts.

ii.

When ghosts enter the forest: birds aflutter
with gossip & hyacinth seeds. Our lives
as trampolines: as vermin who eat &
nest & breed. Our stories on pages made
from old oak bones: our lives as vultures, as
wayfarers on airplane waves. Something's knock-
ing & I don't answer. I know what's there.
Gurgling from the drain: dinner remains
or the last words of my father. Our lives
as parasites on ugly summer days.
Grasshopper: the world goes on without us.

iii.

Billie Holiday at dusk. Her voice a
green balm for all the knives women carry
inside their bones. Waterfalls & wind-spun
days. My father beneath the maple tree

diagramming its roots: unlost & loved.
I smile when I forget he is gone. When
I forget he does not arrive, spectral
& insistent. I sweep sugar red from
the porch. Apply a waterproof layer
to winter wood. Rain is coming. Today.
Tomorrow or next week. A sparrow song.

iv.

A sparrow heartbreak will not stop the flood.

IN WHICH I AM DREAMING ABOUT MY GHOST AGAIN

The ones who stand as tall as windmills: who glow like wolf breath across the field: the ones with runners' bones & beating hearts as loud as a parade. The ones without constraints: embalming fluid: marble names: the ones who speak the language of television without hymns poisoning their veins: my ghosts who never died. My ghosts who never died: the ones who escaped the cemetery of my heart: the ones who packed a suitcase with photographs sliced in half & left my eyes behind: my ghosts who meet in dark bars. My ghosts who meet in dark bars: the ones who floated in my womb like goldfish: like stars: like hurricanes in a coffee cup: like zinnia seeds swept downstream: my hungry ghosts: my hungry ghosts. The ones as full as a pantry: the ones who swallow good bread & ripe tomatoes & sugar as sweet as a train: the ones who smash plates into blades: the ones who carry bouquets: the ones who twirl like ceiling fans: the ones with my love on their lips & fingertips. Daisy chains: my ghosts: my ghosts: my necessary ghosts.

AFTER UVALDE

hungry roots that break through plastic flower

pots wet dirt & worms & petals & yes

the salamander the hawk the first school

dance where i thought i might fall in love &

old telephone booths searching for quarters

& the time we drove into a car wash

& forgot to roll the windows down &

i am tired & hiding & i want

hummingbirds & mockingbirds & morning

lingerie the last three pushes my screams

my daughter breathing against my earlobe

my grandson's arms around my neck the way

he holds on like grass or hunger & you

don't know lightning don't know that when you step

into murky water the unseen things

that scrape or sting or slither around your

ankles are god's pockets emptied I can't

keep reciting all the blooming things you

ought to know can't place pennies on their eyes

i cannot keep counting the dead for you

ALL THE THINGS YOU TRIED TO TELL ME	ALL THE THINGS I ALREADY KNOW
The pink petaled scar on the soft pad of your left foot was not caused by a nail	There are hymns inside our knees that only lightning can hear
You buried your last baby tooth just below the middle toe	Above your hidden freckle
You are your computer's favorite secret	The crows know our secret names and scream them as we pass
You are her softest creation	A strobe light of your hair hello/farewell/hello/farewell /hello
A thesaurus of guillotines etched into your skin	You dreamed of god and buried him
Tulip is always your password	He was too small
Swarms of hummingbirds follow you from room to room from door to garden to mile marker number 72	I thought this would be easier
You have been rejected by algorithms for your failure to provide a number and/or special character	The water was impatient to take you down
Death knows you can float like a swan/a fledgling snake/the newest river of lullabies	There is no difference between the cricket's chirp and the computer's nightly chime

HOW TO KEEP THINGS ALIVE

Golden Shovel with line from The Gun Song by the Lumineers

The wrens first built & second abandoned their petal-lined nest: wilted orange flowers & things

like salamanders & wasps penetrated the thicket of birth. An empty structure still stands & I

am not awakened at 4 am by their riotous song. Listen: I am an accessory to murder. I knew

not to tell anyone: not to shine a flashlight into their home: not a hypothetical scenario when

the outcome is as final as flame. I planted peppermint vines to keep the squirrels away: I

fenced the dahlias with lavender & sage so the rabbits stayed in their patch of clover. I was

planning this violence all winter so everything would open at the same time. Tiger lilies: the young

sparrows rising from their shells. The daisies never stay in chains: they are almost dead. Some

zinnias will last all summer if I can keep the slugs away. I'm learning backyard bird songs: were

you to arrive I could explain the chorus: blue jay / raven / a bright cardinal so true

to his art that his babies will surely be discovered: one by one. Dog-walking neighbors &

rabbit-eating I know this is the circle/I know hunger is a flooded nest/I know. Some

keep their distance today: some look into my window to see what I'm singing: I wish they were

listening without weapons in hand: without teeth or wings: our choices necessary & wrong.

NOTES

CT Salazar — you will recognize the dedication language — as always you say it better than I ever could.

"I'm Inventing a New Language Redux" is in conversation with my poem "I'm Inventing a New Language" which appears in the chapbook *Morning Walk with Dead Possum, Breakfast and Parallel Universe* (Animal Heart Press).

"Flying Doesn't Look Like Flying" is in conversation with my poem "Drowning Doesn't Look Like Drowning" which appears in the chapbook *Morning Walk with Dead Possum, Breakfast and Parallel Universe* (Animal Heart Press).

Some lines from "Requiem" first appeared in the poem "Hydrology (iii)" published in the chapbook *The Water Cycle* (Variant Lit).

"All the Things You Tried to Tell Me / All the Things I Already Know" is dedicated to the beautiful soul and talented poet, artist, musician and friend, Kari Flickinger, who left us too early in 2022. This world will always feel darker without her.

ACKNOWLEDGMENTS

Grateful acknowledgement to the following journals who published some of these poems:

Boats Against the Current — "Something is Waiting to Hatch"

From Parts Unknown: A Pro Wrestling Anthology — "Mutually Assured Destruction"

Many Nice Donkeys — "Full of Grace," "/ Snakeroot/ Oleander / Belladonna /," "sonnets of apology"

Okay Donkey — "In Which I am Dreaming About My Ghosts Again"

Re-Side — "The Spider in the Shower"

Variant Lit — "How to Keep Things Alive"

ABOUT THE AUTHOR

Beth Gordon is a poet, mother, and grandmother currently living in
Asheville, NC. She is the author of *Morning Walk with Dead Possum*,
Breakfast and Parallel Universe (Animal Heart Press), *Particularly
Dangerous Situation* (Clare Songbirds Publishing), *This Small Machine of
Prayer* (Kelsay Books), and *The Water Cycle* (Variant Literature). Beth is
Managing Editor of *Feral: A Journal of Poetry and Art*, Assistant Editor of
Animal Heart Press, and Grandma of Femme Salve Books. You can
find her on Twitter and Instagram @bethgordonpoet.

Made in the USA
Middletown, DE
25 September 2023

39324531R00021